YOUR KNOWLEDGE HAS VALUE

- We will publish your bachelor's and master's thesis, essays and papers

- Your own eBook and book - sold worldwide in all relevant shops

- Earn money with each sale

Upload your text at www.GRIN.com
and publish for free

Bibliographic information published by the German National Library:

The German National Library lists this publication in the National Bibliography; detailed bibliographic data are available on the Internet at http://dnb.dnb.de .

Imprint:

Copyright © 2018 GRIN Verlag
Print and binding: Books on Demand GmbH, Norderstedt Germany
ISBN: 9783668957077

This book at GRIN:

https://www.grin.com/document/465689

Anonym

The Meaning of the Photographs in the Novel "Extremely Loud and Incredibly Close"

GRIN Verlag

GRIN - Your knowledge has value

Since its foundation in 1998, GRIN has specialized in publishing academic texts by students, college teachers and other academics as e-book and printed book. The website www.grin.com is an ideal platform for presenting term papers, final papers, scientific essays, dissertations and specialist books.

Visit us on the internet:

http://www.grin.com/

http://www.facebook.com/grincom

http://www.twitter.com/grin_com

EXTREMELY LOUD AND INCREDIBLY CLOSE

The Meaning of the Photographs in the Novel

Title Page:

Title:	Extremely Loud and Incredibly Close –
	The Meaning of the Photographs in the Novel

Learning Arrangement: PM5 – Effective Communication Skills I

Institute: Fontys International Business School

Course of Studies: International Business and Management Studies

Study Phase: Propaedeutic Phase

Academic Year: 2017 - 2018

Date of completion: 27.04.2018

Spelling: American English

Executive Summary:

In this resume, the whole report will be summarized. The photographs that will be analyzed have been taken out of the novel "Extremely loud and incredibly close", written by Jonathan Safran Foer and became an international bestseller.

The protagonist and simultaneously narrator of the novel Oskar Shell is a nine year old boy who is on a journey to find out the purpose of a key from his deceased father who died in the terrorist attacks on the World Trade Center on September 11, 2001.
Oskar is trying to find out what the left key is for and he is doing that by visiting as many people as he can, with the means of interviewing and photographing them.

The basic aim of this analysis was to achieve a deeper look into Oskar's inside, so that I would gain more information about his character than the written pages in Foer's novel offers.
Moreover, I wanted to prove that most of the chosen photographs which appear in the protagonist's scrapbook, whether they are taken by himself or by others, are connected to Thomas Schell Jr. and underline Oskar's emotional instability after his father's death.
One of my major upcoming questions was if he can escape his difficult past through photographing or if it worsens his fragile condition.

To gain enough knowledge about photography, I skimmed through the book of Susan Sonntag "On Photography" and an applicable newspaper article composed by Jim Richardson about "The View from the Back".
After skimming Sontag's book, I read the novel of Safran again and analyzed the photographs with the help of my existing analyzation skills learned in school and the newly acquired knowledge from the books for my research on photography.

As a result of this analysis, one can say that the chosen analyzed photographs in the scrapbook "Stuff That Happened to Me" let to a broader knowledge about Oskar. Through the photographs he took or printed out from the internet, it becomes clear that Oskar could not get over his beloved father's death, since nearly all of the pictures have something to do with him.
However, they also show that Oskar is a very talented photographer because he respects the wishes of his models. Depending on the model, he either lets them their freedom because he knows about the truthfulness of a picture or he asks them several questions about them, in order to establish a relationship between model and photographer. The photographs also point out that Oskar is very curious and has wide interests, especially in science and in history. If the author had not used photographs in his novel, it would have been more difficult for the reader to relate to Oskar's world, his thoughts and his feelings.

Preface:

In the upcoming section, I am going to explain the aim of this report. The report is written in our PM7 class Effective Communication Skills and is supposed to teach us, the main aspects of writing an academic report.

As the choice of topic was completely our free decision, I decided to write about a topic which I am passionate about, namely about a book.

I chose to compose my report about the meaning of the photographs in the novel "Extremely loud and incredibly close" by Jonathan Safran Foer.

With the help of a book about photography written by Susan Sonntag and an interesting article about photographs from behind from Jim Richardson, I analyzed the importance of the photographs the protagonist of the novel took.

Table of Contents

1. Introduction

In Jonathan Safran Foer's novel "Extremely Loud and Incredibly Close" photographs help the major character, Oskar Schell to document his thoughts and feelings. Oskar is an intelligent and curious boy, so the photographs he collects in a scrapbook named "Stuff That Happened to Me" are rich in diversity.

First there are many pictures which refer directly or indirectly to family members, like his father and his grandfather. Moreover, Oskar collects pictures of people he is not related to but admires a lot, like Stephen Hawking or his cat. The third group of his photographs includes strangers whom the boy briefly or never met at all. Although not every photograph in the novel can be divided into these three groups, I will only focus on selected photographs according to the three groups.

This report will argue that every single group has its own function and reveals different things about Oskar. While photographs connected to his father or grandfather give away something about Oskar's past and his way he of dealing with his loss, the second group, pictures about admired ones helps to become a better image of Oskar's personality and his emotions. The third group that contains photographs of strangers represents his social interaction with foreigners and his interests.

Through analyzing some particular photographs in their contexts, I will achieve a deeper look into Oskar's inside, so that I will gain more information about this character than the written pages in Foer's novel offers.

Moreover, I want to prove that most of the chosen photographs which appear in the protagonist's scrapbook, whether they are taken by himself or by others, are connected to Thomas Schell Jr. and underline Oskar's emotional instability after his father's death.

2. Topic Description

My report for the course "Effective communication skills I" will be about photography in the novel „Extremely Loud and Incredibly Close" by Jonathan Safran Foer.
I will take a look at the protagonist's notebook "Stuff that Happened to Me" and analyze the photos by focusing on their function and their meaning.

Writing about this topic was chosen by me, due to the reason that I read the novel only recently and this book is really inspiring for me and since the picture of the falling man has already been discussed several times, I will rather concentrate on the remaining pictures of the novel, which in my opinion are also extremely meaningful.

First, I will try to find out why the narrator chose these particular photographs and in how far they are connected to the plot. I will examine the relationship between Oskar and the photographed persons, objects or events as well as emotions or thoughts he intends to illustrate with his pictures.
In addition to that, I will determine Oskar's photography technique, what photographing itself means to him, and what he attempts to achieve by collecting pictures in a notebook.

One of my major questions will be if he can escape his difficult past through photographing or if it worsens his fragile condition.

3. Photographs of Characters Oskar Misses
3.1 Oskar's Father

Oskar's interest in photography can be traced back to his intense relationship to his father, Thomas Schell Jr. who died in the attack of 9/11. Father and son had a special bond together, for they did numerous activities together which only included the two of them, like their frequent search for mistakes in the newspaper or special riddles the father asked the child. When Oskar finds a key in an envelope with the name "Black" on it after his father's death, he believes that he found clues for another riddle and wants to find out what the key is for, so he goes on a search. His camera accompanies him throughout the whole quest, in order to document his results. The hunt after the lock becomes very important to Oskar because he now feels connected to his father whom he misses a lot, "Every time I left our apartment to go searching for the lock, I became a little lighter, because I was getting closer to Dad" (Foer 2012: 52).
The photographs show that he is trying hard to find the answer and fulfill his father's expectations. In the past when the father riddled his son, Oskar had always shown his progress in detail to his parent and was excited about his reaction, "'Here's what I've found,' I said, pushing my pussy off the table with the tray of evidence. [...] 'Can't you even tell me if I'm on the right track?'" (Foer 2012: 9).
After the father's death, the child wants to hold on to this tradition, thus he keeps collecting evidences of his search. However; he does not want to show his efforts of the current investigation to anyone else, not even his mother because solving riddles had always been a father-son action. The boy replaces the real evidences with pictures of them, for he wants to hold his father up to date and aims to make him proud, because according to Susan Sontag (1977: 3) "Photographs furnish evidence ".

Most of the photographs in the novel, at least the ones Oskar takes during his search after the lock, are in some way related to Thomas Schell Jr. Yet there are two pictures in "Stuff That Happened to Me" which Oskar explicitly connects to his deceased father. The first one is a shot of a tennis player from the newspaper Thomas Schell Jr. read the day before he was killed. Cutting this photograph out of the news and pasting it into his book, is an attempt to feel his father's nearness, to touch what he touched before. The photograph was cut out of a newspaper which plays a striking role in the father- son relationship and brings back fond memories of his father, due to the reason that they used to search together for mistakes in it.

The second essential photograph about Thomas Schell Jr. is a picture of a man from behind. Oskar photographed this stranger because he reminded him of his father. He cannot fully accept that his father is dead; therefore, keeps on searching and seeing his face everywhere. After the September 11 attacks, Oskar continues to seek for clues about his father's fate. On the one hand he looks at several videos and pictures on the internet to find actual proof of his father's death, on the other hand he uses his fantasy to speculate about the many possible ways his father could have died, "You saw in some of the pictures that people jumped together and held hands. So maybe they did that" (Foer 2012: 196).

3.2 Oskar's Grandfather

The other person who is strongly connected to Oskar's photography is his grandfather, even though Oskar never met him consciously. The camera the protagonist always carries with him belonged to his grandfather and is very important to the boy. Every time when Oskar pulls out the camera to take a picture with it, he refers to it as "grandpa's camera" (Foer 2012: 99).

After the grandfather learned that his son was one of the victims of the terroristic attacks on 9/11, he returns home and finally gets to know his grandchild.
Oskar however, does not know that the silent, old man whom he accidently met is related to him. Nevertheless, Oskar immediately decides to trust him because he is fascinated by him, especially by his hands which are tattooed with the words "YES" and "NO", out of this reason he takes a picture of them and puts it into his scrapbook.
Before he photographs the hands, Oskar asks his grandpa -only known as the renter to him- questions about his tattoos, for instance "But why just YES and NO?" [...] "What about 'I'll think about it' and 'probably' and 'it's possible'?" (Foer 2012: 257). These questions show that Oskar is very interested in his models and wants to know everything about them before taking pictures. This corresponds with Susan Sontag's claim that "To photograph is to appropriate the thing photographed. It means putting oneself into a certain relation to the world that feels like knowledge-and, therefore, like power" (Sontag 1977: 2).
In this sense, photography can be seen as an appropriate hobby for Oskar because he is curious, eager to know and is not shy to ask questions.
Despite the fact that Oskar does not get to know his grandfather until the age of nine they have a lot in common. Oskar permanently uses the camera his grandpa left behind, because they share a common interest in photography. The grandfather used to take pictures of doorknobs, an act that is met with incomprehension by his wife, "He took a picture of every doorknob in the apartment. Everyone. As if the world and its future depended on each doorknob. As if we would be thinking about doorknobs should we ever actually need to use the pictures of them" (Foer 2012: 175). Thomas Schell Sr. took those pictures, so he and his wife would be able to rebuild their apartment if anything happened.
Like Oskar he collected the photographs in a book that he always took with him. He feared that an accident might destroy the unique order he and his wife established together and wanted everything to remain the same, since he is unable to deal with changes. For the same reason, he left his wife when she became pregnant. As it can be seen in numerous passages in the novel, the elder Thomas Schell is traumatized by the past, as he survived the bombing of Dresden where his girlfriend was killed, henceforth he is afraid of loss. The doorknobs, on which he is focusing so much, can be understood as the repressed impulse to go and leave everything behind.
His grandson is also very interested in doors and takes pictures of them during his search after the matching lock to his key. Just as his grandfather, Oskar has to deal with a difficult past because he also lost a person he loved. His pictures of doors show his progress in finding clues for the riddle his father gave to him. Taking pictures of the large amount of possible locks in New York City demonstrates his strong will and his love for his father. "I tried the key in all of the doors, even though he said he didn't recognize it [...] It's that at the end of my search I wanted to be able to say: I don't know how I could have tried harder" (Foer 2012: 160).
All in all, Oskar's father and grandfather are very important for analyzing the photographs in the novel because the child feels inspired and motivated by them. With his photos he aims to keep the relationship upright and feels connected to both of them. Many of the pictures in the

novel are related to the young and the old Thomas Schell; they reflect Oskar's happy memories as well as his sad emotions.

4. Photographs of Characters, Oskar Admires
4.1. Stephen Hawking

There is another male character that plays a striking role in Oskar's life, namely the physicist Stephen Hawking. Oskar is very impressed by him and refers numerous times to him. He also imitates his significant voice sometimes, asks himself in difficult situations what Hawking would do in his position and Hawking's "A Brief History of Time" is Oskar's favorite book; he reads it all the time. Hawking functions as an idol for Oskar, who calls himself an "amateur astronomer" (Foer 2012: 99).

To show his admiration, the nine-year-old writes many fan letters to Stephen Hawking. "I thought he wasn't going to respond, because he was such an amazing person and I was so normal" (Foer 2012: 11). In fact, he only receives automatic replies with Hawking's promise to answer soon. It takes the astrophysicist two years to respond appropriately, but he finally writes a very personal and honest letter back to him. Oskar however, never comments on the letters he receives from him. The reader does not learn whether Oskar is disappointed by the automatic replies or glad about the personal one. The boy writes letters to other famous scientists as well; asking them to be their assistant, nonetheless Hawking is the only one whose photograph appears in "Stuff that Happened to Me".

This photograph is interesting, because it is no ordinary portrait of Stephen Hawking. Oskar chose a picture of him where his face is seen through a camera. This could be a hint that he secretly wishes to be the one who took that specific photo and encourages his imagination that he one day could meet and then take a picture of his idol with his own camera. Moreover, the photograph is tiny, and Hawking seems a bit helpless because he does not look into the camera. Oskar decided to put this picture in his notebook, for it fits his image of the physicist. When he learned about the Hawking's illness, he asks him in a letter if he could be his "protégé" (Foer 2012: 11). Here it becomes clear that Oskar conceives a strong affection for Hawking and tries to protect him, because he does not want to lose him like he lost his father. The protagonist feels guilty for his father's death and believes that he failed to protect him. He does not want to repeat that mistake, so he offers Hawking his protection.

4.2. Oskar's Cat

Oskar's cat, named after the famous inventor Buckminster Fuller is also crucial to Oskar. There is a photograph of it in "Stuff That Happened to Me" where the cat jumps out of a window. The fact that the cat is jumping shows that Oskar is curious and interested in physics, as he explains to his classmates how "[…] cats reach terminal velocity by making themselves into little parachutes […]" (Foer 2012: 190). This photograph is, like many others also connected to Oskar's father who might have jumped out of the World Trade Center. The cat and the experiment represent Oskar's wish that his father could have survived falling from so many floors, like his cat did. This allusion becomes clearer if one compares the photograph of the falling cat with those of the falling man which appear several times in his collection. He captured the photograph in this dangerous moment because it makes him proud of his cat and reminds him of his father's death.

However, the fall is not the only connection between his father and his pet. Buckminster is always there when Oskar talks about his father. For instance, he pushed it of the table to show his father the evidences of his search, or he petted it while he was listening to his father's last messages on the answering machine before he died. Buckminster is Oskar's best friend and he loves it a lot because it was always there for him. "[…] Buckminster's paws were on my eyelids. He must have been feeling my nightmares" (Foer 2012: 74) is another passage where the intense relationship to the animal and Oskar's trust in it are outlined.

Both Hawking and Buckminster appear in Oskar's scrapbook to illustrate his affection and interest in them. He is fascinated by both of them and mentions them very often. The photographs show Oskar's passion for physics but do also represent his stubbornness and dreams for the future related to Hawking. The pictures also show vulnerability and Oskar's compulsion to protect them. He perpetuates the astrophysicist and the cat in "Stuff That Happened to Me" because he wants to memorize them. In this sense, the two pictures also relate to Thomas Schell Jr. because after his father's death Oskar is worried that he will lose other loved ones, too.

5. Photographs of Characters Oskar Superficially Knows
5.1 Abby Black

Oskar does not always take pictures of people he admires or whom he knows for a long time. There are also a few photographs of people he previously met, like the one of Abby Black, a young woman Oskar meets during his search after the lock and spends some time with. The picture of her is peculiar and different from the others, because it shows Mrs. Black from behind. Although the woman agreed that Oskar could take a photograph of her, she covers her face as soon as Oskar raised his camera. The boy does not mind "I did not want to force her to explain herself, so I thought of a different picture I could take, which would be more truthful, anyway" (Foer 2012: 99).
Oskar acts sensibly, since he saw Mrs. Black crying before and can understand how she is feeling. He is content with this position from behind because he knows that a picture of her smiling face would hide the truth, that the woman is actually unhappy. The smile would have been forced; therefore, they come to the compromise of a picture that shows only the back from Abby Black's head.
The photojournalist Jim Richardson confirms "Images taken from the back have a different quality. Without the faces these pictures become insights into humanity" (Richardson 2011). Despite his young age Oskar seems to understand a lot about photography and how to interact best with his models. He intuitively does the right thing and respects the wishes of people he is photographing. Once again, he proves that he is extremely mature for a nine-year-old.

5.2. Two Cavemen and an Astronaut

However; like many children at this age, Oskar is really interested in the world and its development from the very beginning to the present. One can find pictures of historical significance in "Stuff That Happened to Me" which Oskar himself could not have taken because he was too young then. There is, for instance, a picture of two cavemen in the snow, or one of a French astronaut, surrounded by the press. These two pictures are very diverse, for they both represent another time period. While the cavemen mark the beginnings of human history, the astronaut is a symbol for human development and scientific progress. Oskar put both pictures in his scrapbook, because he is interested in history, science and the human body, which becomes clear when he talks about "the picture of Jean- Pierre Haigneré, the French astronaut who had to be carried from his spacecraft after returning from the Mir station, because gravity isn't only what makes us fall, it's what makes our muscles stronger" (Foer 2012: 243).
It is striking that Oskar did not choose a picture on the internet where the astronaut is depicted as a hero in a space shuttle; instead the child pasted a photograph in his book which shows the astronaut in a weak moment. Oskar wanted to point out that human beings are inferior to nature. Moreover, he is fascinated by the fact that people do not always have control over their bodies or their fate, which can be interpreted as an allusion to his father's sudden death. In a world without his father Oskar feels helpless, overstrained and unprotected, like the astronaut in the picture when he came back to a world with gravity. In brief, Oskar's photographs of strangers help to understand Oskar better because one gets more information on Oskar's character and behavior. Those pictures prove that Oskar is a very empathic as well as talented and interested in various topics.

6. Conclusion

Oskar Schell's scrapbook "Stuff That Happened to Me" is a good mean for the reader to gain an insight into the narrator's world. The pictures this term paper was dealing with, were divided into three groups; pictures standing in relationship to family members he misses, pictures of the ones he admires and pictures of people he briefly or never met. Every category has its own function and is crucial for understanding the protagonist better. The first group reflected his past, the second his emotions and the last one his interests.

Through the photographs the protagonist takes, the reader learns something about his problems in dealing with his father's death. He misses his father and his grandfather as well, although he never met them. Both men have a strong influence on Oskar's photography and he shoots pictures of people and things that remind him of his father, so that he can remember the good memories he shared with him. Furthermore, Oskar unknowingly photographs the same objects as his grandfather, namely doors, because they both had to overcome the death of a loved person and try to move on.

In addition to that, the reader gets to know Oskar more through the pictures he takes of admired ones, like Stephen Hawking or his cat Buckminster. It becomes clear how strong willed and guarding Oskar can be, in order to protect them.

The third group, photographs of people he shortly or never contacted, like Abby Black or two cavemen reflect on the one side Oskar's social competence and his sensitivity, on the other side his interests in the world and its history.

After the thorough analyze, it becomes clear that these three groups certainly expose three different things about Oskar; however, they often overlap and complement each other. By examining the second group which included photographs of characters he admires, it became clear that there is also a link to the first group, of characters he misses. Because Oskar admires Hawking and his cat so much, he is simultaneously afraid of losing them, like he lost his father and grandfather. The cat reminds him of his father because it has always been there when he was with his him. Furthermore, the second group can also be connected to the third one, due to the reason that the photographs of Hawking and the cat also prove Oskar's interest in science. In this sense, it completes the third group of photographs that was originally about the boy's interests and affections. Hence, the three groups bring together and confirm the same facts, characteristics, and qualities of Oskar.

Another noticeable fact is that Oskar often tends to depict people in his photographs as helpless, endangered or weak. Instead of using favorable portraits of those famous people, the pictures in Oskar's scrapbook show the astrophysicist Hawking and the astronaut Haigneré in extraordinary situations where they look defenseless. Since Oskar is a strongly empathetic child, he feels with them and wants to help or protect them. Moreover, Oskar can identify with these photographs because after his father's death he also feels helpless and scared because he lost his father as his protector.

To sum up, one can say that the chosen analyzed photographs in the scrapbook "Stuff That Happened to Me" let to a broader knowledge about Oskar. Through the photographs he took or printed out from the internet, it becomes clear that Oskar could not get over his beloved father's death, since nearly all of the pictures have something to do with him.

However, they also show that Oskar is a very talented photographer because he respects the wishes of his models. Depending on the model, he either lets them their freedom because he knows about the truthfulness of a picture or he asks them several questions about them, in order to establish a relationship between model and photographer. The photographs also point out that Oskar is very curious and has wide interests, especially in science and in history. If the author had not used photographs in his novel, it would have been more difficult for the reader to relate to Oskar's world, his thoughts and his feelings.

7. Critical Appraisal

At the end of this report, a critical look on the execution and problems of this task will be given.

First of all, this report cannot be taken as an excellent analyzation of photographs in novels, due to the reason that this is my first approach in writing a report and also the cause that this report was not established for publication, but only for a training purpose and I am neither a skilled book critic nor a photographer.
During my first writing approach, I was astonished about the format, especially about the little line spacing and realized for the first time how huge the extent of the report had to be and that I had to start writing as soon as possible to finish in time. To help the students writing their reports, a well formulated example report on any topic would be good to have as a model.

Combined with the two other tasks we had to hand in for the Effective Communication course, it became quite time-consuming to finish each task properly at the set deadlines. That is why I would suggest decreasing the course tasks to one or two main tasks, but not three, as this is arduous to agree with the workload of the other courses we have in university.

Reference List

Books

Foer, J. S. F. (2012). Extremely Loud & Incredibly Close. London, England: Penguin.

Sontag, S.S. (1977) *On Photography.* New York, USA: Farrar, Straus and Giroux

Online article

Richardson, J. R. (2011, March 15). The View from the Back. Retrieved May 7, 2018, from https://www.nationalgeographic.com/photography/photo-tips/view-from-the-back-richardson/

Appendix

3. Photographs of Characters Oskar Misses

3.1 Oskar's Father

A stranger, who reminds
Oskar of his father

Tennis player from the newspaper
Thomas Schell Jr. read the day
before he was killed

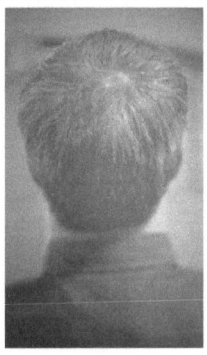

3.2 Pictures that are connected to Oskar's Grandfather

Hands of his grandfather he
photographed

Doorknobs, Oskar and his
grandfather both like to photograph

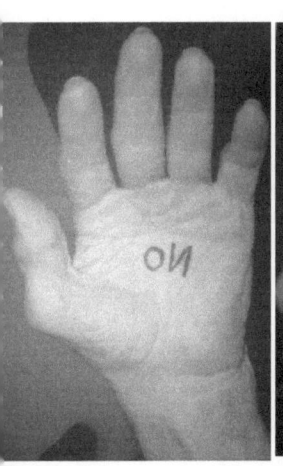

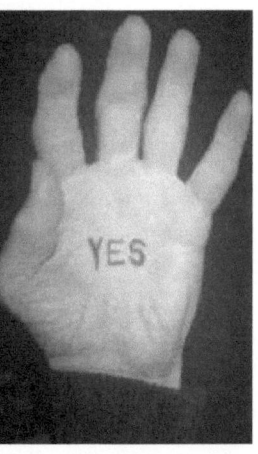

4. Photopgraphs of Characters Oskar Admires

4.1. Stephen Hawking

Stephen Hawking through a camera

4.2. Oskar's Cat

Oskar's Cat Buckminster

5. Photographs of Characters Oskar Superficially Knows

5.1 Abby Black

Abby Black photographed
from behind

5.2. Two Cavemen and an Astronaut

The french astronaut Jean- Pierre
Haigneré in a weak moment

two cavemen in the snow